Poems, Prayers and Other Propaganda

To Help You Make It Through the Night

Margaret A. Gilbert

Edited by Claude R. Royston

BK Royston Publishing LLC

Jeffersonville, IN

BK Royston Publishing
P. O. Box 4321
Jeffersonville, IN 47131
502-802-5385
http://bkroystonpublishing.com
bkroystonpublishing@gmail.com

Published by: BK Royston Publishing LLC
Cover Design: Customwebchoice.com

ISBN-13: 978-0692323441
ISBN-10: 0692323449

Printed in the United States of America

Acknowledgement

Writing is a gift for some, a passion for others and a spirit filled called for people like me. No matter what pulls you into the writing arena, you need a support group.

A very special thank you goes to my husband Tommy who has been the wind beneath my wings. Without his support and encouragement it would have been impossible for me to complete my first book. His understanding nature allowed me to steal away whenever I needed to escape into the wonderful world of putting pin to paper and wonder down poetry lane at my leisure.

It is my older sister Patricia Massey who is my rock, my sounding board and my accountability partner. She is an awesome example of service to others and she gives me the courage to continue on even when I can't see the forest for the trees. Thanks Ms. Massey for being an example that has inspired me to look at writing as a gift from God to share with my fellowman.

To my Pastor, Apostle Amos L. Howard, Sr. who is the person I have to credit for pushing me to actually finish this project. His unrelenting faith in my ability made it impossible for me to quit. His heart filled sermons always give me inspiration for another poem.

To my daughter, April Wood who gave me the idea to publish a book in the first place. She and my grandchildren and great-grandchildren are the subject of many of my writings. Just watching their day to day interactions should provide me with enough subject matter to keep me going for years to come.

To God, who graced me with the courage to complete this work, the tenacity to continue in the face of many challenges and the wisdom to allow His spirit to speak to me and through me using poetry as the instrument of His Voice.

GGGIRL

Dedication

This book is dedicated to God the Father for giving me the grace to finish this project and be an unselfish representative of his love and to my husband, Tommy Gilbert, for loving me as Christ loved the church and for giving me the freedom, support, patience and courage to be obedient to God's will.

GGGirl

.

INTRODUCTION

My poetry has been a work in progress for many years. The Poems started out as quotes or sayings to encourage others. As a child, I remembered sayings or "old wives tales" that older persons would use to get their point across. For example, "a stitch in time saves nine". Or "prior proper planning prevents poor performance". These words of wisdom were used to encourage you not to procrastinate or put chores off for another time.

I first started making up my own personal sayings after I became a supervisor in the Military as a way of encouraging my airmen to stay the course and not quit. Of course, the military itself has many acronyms and cadences that were used in our drill ceremonies. For instance, I would use rhymes to help my airmen remember the "orders of the officers appointed over them". Words like "stick to the task until it sticks to you, bend with it, cry with it until you see it through" helped to encourage them not to quit. These short sayings eventually developed into poems.

This collection of poetry is God's way of speaking to me and through me when I find myself, or others who are encountering difficult situation. There are times when they help me better understand the message of a sermon. Once I put the message in the form of a poem, I gain clearer revelation of what has been said.

If I am listening for an answer to a particular question from God or direction on what to do or how to navigate a situation, He will plant a poem in my spirit that gives me a better understanding of what action to take. Sometimes the poem is simply a word from God that eases my troubled heart and reminds me that He is near.

Isaiah 50:4 (NIV) says, "The Sovereign Lord has given me a well-instructed tongue, to know the word that sustains the weary". That word from me is through poetry. This collection of poems is a way for me to communicate empathy for others. I pray that the lyrics will warm persons' hearts, bring inspiration and encouragement during difficult times and most of all give them peace in the midst of their storms.

Table of Contents

Let's Go to Church

A Tribute to My Pastor 1

Can God Trust You With a 2
Tragedy

Free In Christ 4

Generation Truth 5

Has Your Love Waxed Cold 7

It's Giving Time 9

I Made A Pact With God 10

Living in The Super Natural From 11
the Sermon By Apostle Amos L.
Howard, Sr.

Mary's Song – Luke 1:46 12

Meet God In Faith 14

My Birthday Wish to the Faith 15
Fighter

Oh Give Thanks Unto The Lord 17

Pentecost 19

Put Your Armor On 21

The Privilege of Giving 23

It's A Family Affair

A Mother's Love 24

A Mother's Love II 26

A Tribute to Sister 27

April Showers Bring May Flowers 28

Are You Who He Wants to Be 30

Black Beauty 31

Come Remember With Me 32

My Friend   36

Encouragement

Courage   38
Death To Self   39
Don't Ask Me to Suffer   40
Don't Open the Gates   43
Dream On   44
Eat More – Payless   46
How Do You Keep the Smile   48
I Am Here   50
I Asked The Lord to Bless You   52
I Prayed For You   53
I Wish You Enough   54
It's Okay to Be Okay   55
Jesus On You   58
Moving Forward   59
My Wish For You   60
No Hill For a Climber   61

Military Related

An American Man   63
Military Woman   65

America

911 In Review   67
A Black Man in The White House   70
Change in America   72

A Tribute to My Pastor

- God is not a man that he should lie – for your freedom he did die.
- You are free to live and learn – from his word never turn.
- You were created as God's best – the world will have to deal with the rest.
- You are the righteousness of God – His favorite son – let his will for your life always be done.
- Go forth – dominate – conquer and subdue – that is why he created you.
- No weapon formed against you will pass – no anger – jealousy – or wrong will last.
- God surrounds you with favor because of your righteous behavior.
- Your love for him is so great – He will never leave you at the gate.
- He will stick by you through thick and then – with him by your side you will always win.
- You are the head and not the tail – you sit high and look low. Remember to take him with you wherever you go.
- So fight for your grades – focus on your goals – Remember "I AM" sent you and your victory is yet to unfold!

CAN GOD TRUST YOU WITH A TRAGEDY?

Can he allow a tear to fall from your eye?

And know that your smile will brighten the sky?

Can He know that when your goals aren't met

That you will shine and still him represent?

If you are the one without the thing

Can you still His heavenly praises sing?

When life's circumstances don't go your way

Will you be the one to continue to pray?

Will you not grieve when the enemy seems to win?

Can He see His face in your heart and His love in your grin?

Will you be the one with the giving heart.

When all those around you are falling apart?

Will He be able to point at you.

And say to the world this is what you should do?

Don't be afraid to suffer in His name

For when you do you are already ahead in the game.

FREE IN CHRIST

The day He laid upon that tree was the day Christ set me free

The day they nailed His hands and feet was the day I released defeat

The day they pierced Him in the side was the day my sins died

Never to rise and claim me again – the day my new life began!

The day they put a crown on His head was the day I rose from my barren bed

The day He drank from the bitter cup – is the day I learned to always look up

To free my soul from death and despair- and receive a love that cannot compare

To anything I'd ever known – to be free in Christ and never again be alone.

GENERATION TRUTH

- Our Generation it's the Balm – The blessed gift of our Lord who keeps us calm!
- The now generation, we stand for God – we are his voice – He is expecting great things – so we have no choice.
- GT
- No weapon formed against us shall prosper because God is our guide – we're going to spread his message nationwide.
- Our leaders are alive, that ain't no jive they teach us how to keep our hope alive.
- GT
- Pastor Linda feeds us the word. She is the most powerful speaker we have ever heard!
- She brings us life through speaking the truth – she brings us hope and we have proof -- we are living, breathing truth.
- GT
- We hear the word – we store it in our spirit - So when we need it – we are always near it.
- GT – GREAT THINGS – I like how that rings - Only Great things come from our team.
- This is our season – this is our time – Great things for his reason – and that ain't just a line.
- GT
- The now generation for the world today - Stop and listen to what we have to say
- Our message is clear – we fight for Jesus without any fear
- The future is ours – we'll take it without toil - We'll conquer every inch of this old earth's soil.
- GT

- We'll spread the good news of his love to all - We'll show the world how not to fall.
- We stand for God, we are his voice - We are his ambassador's by choice.
- GT
- As we move to our next work for Jesus Christ – we'll love him forever because of his awesome sacrifice!
- GT

HAS YOUR LOVE WAXED COLD?

You've lost that loving feeling

- You no longer find Him appealing. The world has deceived you into drinking from its selfish cup. Get rid of that stinking thinking – come back to your first love – The one straight from above.
- You've tasted from the cup of lust – you've gotten your fill and it seems that you will burst. From selfish gain to greed and fame – you really think you've got the hang of their game. You wine and dine and dress so fine – You stole from Him who originally made you shine.
- His love was faithful and true. This new fellow is making a fool out of you. He tells you lies that turn your head – So why do you now feel like you are dead? You have no life – you're always in strife. Every waking moment is a struggle.
  You don't know whether to come or go. There are no principles involved – it's all just for show.
- Come back to the one who loved you most. Come back to the place that allowed you to boast. A love that can see you through – no matter what circumstances are laid on you. He'll never leave you or forsake you – He won't shame you or try to blame you. He'll get your slack when the world turns its back.

- He'll love you and keep you safe in his arms.
  No longer will that old flame do you harm.
- He will greet you with love honor – no matter
  what you've done. The focus will be you – You
  are his one and only one.
- The love of his life – He's your husband –
  You're his wife!
  You'll be able to start again –

WELCOME HOME MY DEAR FRIEND!

IT'S GIVING TIME!!!!!!

THIS IS THE TIME TO GIVE SOME MORE

YOUR HOUSE OF SEED HE WILL RESTORE!

HE IS LOOKING FOR A PLACE TO LAND TO FIND SOME BORDERS TO EXPAND!

SEEK YE FIRST HIS KINGDOM HE SAID – THE CHILDREN OF GOD WILL NEVER BE WITHOUT BREAD!

YOUR NEEDS HE KNOWS – NO LACK NO SHAME

IT'S THROUGH HIS SON'S LOVE THAT YOU WIN THE GAME!

KEEP GIVING AND LIVING – LONG LIFE IS FOR SURE

YOUR POCKETS WILL STAY FULL AND YOUR HEART WILL STAY PURE.

I MADE A PACT WITH GOD

- I made a pact with God today – I told Him I heard what He had to say
- I'd made up my mind to serve the Divine the way I was supposed to do.
- I repented for not being obedient for not following His ways
- I made up my mind to leave sin behind and do whatever He says
- The world had blinded me – took me aside, showed me a life
- That looked like my guide.
- My spirit said no – but my flesh made me go – to a place I had never been
- It looked good from afar but my soul knew it was sin
- I thought money, and folly were all that mattered to me
- But life taught me lessons about how ugly disobedience could be
- I asked God to forgive me to lead me back. I wanted to get my life back on track.
- I vowed to give Him my heart as well as my hand. I vowed never again to serve sinful man
- I'll take up His cross and carry it well – I'll send old Satan straight back to hell.
- I'll never again leave home to find the beautiful life that was already mine.
- So make the vow to serve Him again – you'll never have a more trusted friend.

LIVING IN THE SUPER NATURAL FROM THE SERMON BY
Apostle Howard

- God has called us to the supernatural for such a time as this.
- To live with him untouched by man in a state of perfect bliss
- Sweat less victories, no more toil – stepping out beyond the spoils
- The first act requires a leap of faith – walking in purpose – focusing on His gait.
- Although it may not be your turn – it is your time you see – step right in and be all that you can be
- So drop the concerns – only focused action will get you to your turn
- If you admit it – it is your time to use what you have got – so don't wait - move on to the right spot
- God has done all that He promised – He has released his word
- If you want to walk on water just do what you have heard

Mary's Song Luke 1:46

- There is a song that Mary sang – it glorifies the Lord's name

- My spirit rejoices in God my savior because he shows me so much favor

- This song she sings is mindful of the humble state I'm in – of how the Lord used me even - when I was in sin

- From now on all generations will call me blessed - the song says He will do nothing less

- This one thing I must confess the mighty One has done great things -Holy is his name!

- His mercy extends to those who fear him – from this generation on –He has performed magnificent deeds – His arms have kept me strong

- Her son says he filled the hungry with good things – her voice so sweet as she sings

- It helps me remember He was merciful to Abraham and his descendants because it is on His GRACE that they were dependent

- He raised up the humble and brought down rulers from their thrones

- He scattered those who are proud in their thought and lifted up his own

- Her song has stayed with me – it lifted my head as high as the tree, it opened my heart and brought me back to thee.

MEET GOD IN FAITH

When your faith meets God's faithfulness – Jesus will show up. Expect him to show up and then drink from his cup.

He will show up in you; in those you meet on the street too

 Be vigilant – expect him soon - seek him and he will show up before noon.

Lift Jesus up as you go on your way. Lift him up and He will show up for you today!!!

MY BIRTHDAY WISH TO THE FAITH FIGHTER

I AM FIFTY-EIGHT AND I'M FEELING GREAT
God's mercy and grace keeps me in this race.

When I doubted during evil's flood
I found comfort in His mighty word.

He kept me safe within His arms
And shielded me from all hurt and harm.

He removed the clouds from my life
And gave me peace during periods of strife.

I bless the Lord for all his Joy
Especially His loving baby boy!

I praise His name because He choose me to
fellowship with you
And I thank you daily for all you do!

I lift my hands in heavenly praise
To be able to share with you these blessed days.

You build me up when I'm feeling down
And help me stay on solid ground!

You've made my journey a whole lot brighter
And I will always treasure you – my fellow
Faith Fighters!

OH GIVE THANKS UNTO THE LORD

I give thanks unto THEE – for all you've done for me

I give thanks from my very soul – that by thy might will never grow cold

I give thanks for every breath I breathe – for through His grace and mercy I receive

Every blessing for which I have faith to believe

OH give thanks unto the Lord for He is good – He treats me like a precious father should!

His grace and mercy endure for ever – Please don't leave me – please don't –not ever!

I give thanks for everything – no matter what the circumstance

I give thanks because His love is not by chance.

He knew me before I was formed

He knew that through him no one could do me harm.

OH GIVE THANKS!

I give thanks for his Son – Because of Him my battle is already won!

I will extol you Oh God everyday

I give thanks for your faithful way

I thank you for peaceful living

Oh my God – Your love just keeps on giving!

My mouth shall speak of Your wonders and gratefully praise Your Holy name

I give thanks to You and You alone because of You I know no shame!

OH GIVE THANKS!

I give thanks for Your love so true

Without it what in the world would I do?

OH GIVE THANKS!

I give thanks because You are my joy.

I give thanks like a kid with a brand new toy.

I praise Your name every day – I praise Your glory in a special way.

I give thanks for the opportunity to worship You

It takes me to that secret place – so high I can see Your face.

OH GIVE THANKS!

I give thanks for all of Your peace – I give thanks because it will never cease

It wraps me in tender loving care

I give thanks because You are always there.

OH GIVE THANKS

No matter when – no matter where

I will always give thanks because I know You care!

PENTECOST

THE DAY OF PENTECOST IS OUR APPOINTED TIME TO MEET WITH THE GREAT I AM- THE BLOOD OF THE LAMB.

IT IS A SPECIAL DIVINE INITATION TO EVERY MAN WOMAN AND CHILD IN EVERY NATION

WE CANNOT AFFORD TO MISS OUR DATE FOR IT CONTROLS OUR VERY FATE

IT IS A TIME WHEN WE RECEIVE THE POWER THE ANOINTING THE PROMISE OF THE HOLY SPIRIT

IT IS THE PROMISE OF THE LORD – NO NEED TO FEAR IT

THE DOOR IS OPEN FOR YOU TO RECEIVE IF YOU JUST HAVE FAITH AND BELIEVE

SO DON'T MISS OUT BECAUSE OF DOUBT, DISTRUST AND FEAR.

GOD'S FAVOR AND BLESSINGS ARE CLOSE – THEY ARE NEAR

FALL DOWN HOLY SPIRIT AND RAIN ON ME

FILL ME WITH THE POWER OF THEE

WHEN WE FALL IN WORSHIP AND GO UP IN PRAISE

WE WELCOME YOU IN WITH A LOVE FILLED HEART AND HOLY HANDS RAISED

WE THANK YOU FOR THE PRIVILEGE OF MEETING YOU TODAY

FOR ALLOWING US TO COMMUNE WITH YOU AND PRAY

WE THANK YOU FOR PROSPERITY, PROMOTION, PROVISION, GRACE AND PEACE

FOR GIVING US SOME TIME TO MEET YOU FACE TO FACE.

FREE FROM A LEGACY AND LINEAGE OF CURSE, PAIN AND DISGRACE

NO THIS GENERATION IS ANEW WITH LIFE AND WILL WIN THE RACE

FREE TO DANCE AND SING FREE TO LIFT MY HANDS IN WORSHIP TO HONOR THEE--

TO PRAISE YOUR MIGHTY NAME – AND KNOW MY WALK WAS NOT IN VAIN

THANK YOU THAT I AM FREE AND I WILL NEVER BE BOUND AGAIN.

THANK YOU THAT I AM FREE AND I WILL NEVER BE BOUND AGAIN!

PUT YOUR ARMOR ON

There's A war Going on

- There is a war going on – there's some "Spiritual Static". I can't hear from God – I'm feeling like a worldly addict.

- I changed the channel because I couldn't hear – the word of God in my inner ear.

- We must go through some spiritual warfare to get a clear word – Satan disguised as my flesh has jammed my reception and scrambled what I heard.

- He told me to feed my desires, my reason and my emotions – I clearly understood. It felt so good it had to be a Godly notion.

- The enemy – my fleshly voice said to give them whatever they wanted – But I knew that doing so would cause my Spirit voice to be taunted.

- We know they stay at odds with each other – sort of like little sister and big brother.

- They exist together – but not on the same accord. Their wires are crossed – so my feelings had to get on board.

- The static was cleared by the word of God. But I had to keep it close buried in my heart.

- I bound those feelings and sense of reason – God is now the channel for my every season.

- The Holy Spirit has come to aide me - to teach me all things – God's principals are now my king.

- He always speaks to me according to His will for my life. The steps of a good man are ordered with no toil or strife.

- I must seek your face God to hear your voice – so take me to your perfect place of choice.

- I expect the voice to be clear and precise. I need clear communication to keep my life off that slippery ice.

- Stay tuned – be vigilant – be on purpose for Him – then that channel will be clear and concise and your life not so dreary and dim.

THE PRIVILEGE OF GIVING

THANK YOU GOD FOR THE PRIVILEGE OF GIVING

I AM SOWING MY SEED

I AM PLANTING IT FAST

I AM SOWING IT OFTEN

SO THAT MY BLESSINGS WILL LAST

HELP ME TO REMEMBER TO

GIVE ALL GLORY TO YOU

BECAUSE WITHOUT YOU WHAT WOULD I DO.

A Mother's Love

A mother's love is always near, it removes our hurt and calms our fear.

It gives us what we need at the very time it is due. It will correct, encourage and strengthen you.

Your mother can never be replaced, she was given through God's unmerited grace.

Your friends sometimes don't understand how one person can mean so much.

That's because they have not felt the gentleness of her touch.

She is the one who offers the helping hand to hold, when in life we seem to drown.

She's the one we can count on despite what's going down.

The person who is there no matter where you are,

in the valley or on the mountain top, whether you are near or far.

She'll stick with you no matter what step you find yourself on.

Especially when all those fickle unfaithful friends are gone.

God made mothers to bring us into this world, to nurture, encourage and inspire us.

Her time is spent in preparing us for God's appointed purpose.

Mothers are those creatures who love us to prepare us to leave you know

They guide us down life's path so that we can walk successfully through life's door.

If we listen to and follow through, we'll inherit God's Kingdom here on earth

And in the end be able to find our own self-fulfilling worth.

A MOTHER'S LOVE II

A mother's love is sent from above

Wrapped in a heart of gold.

It's the kind of love that stays by your side

The kind that never grows old.

It brings the kind of joy of dreams.

It cares and cries and smothers it seems

But once you know it and feel its touch

You'll know why a mother means so much.

You are our gift our reward for good

We would keep you all to ourselves if we could.

But sharing your love is what you do

So here is my love to share with you!

A Tribute to Sister

Fun-loving and tenacious.

Good hearted and caring. Her smile lit up the room.

Always there in times of need, to others she never
brought gloom.

A friend in need is a friend in deed was what she
would always say.

A sister for life, a friend to the end – she always
brightened your day.

Though gone in the flesh her spirit lingers on

Through the thought of her bird-like songs!

We cherished her gift from God above and remember
her graciously with love.

April Showers Bring May Flowers

April my love– you are as smooth as your name sake and just as fair. Like a soft breeze blowing in my ear – spreading words of wisdom so dear.

Just like small animals that hibernate but come out of their burrows in April – people come out to hear your words of wisdom – for you are so faithful!

The birds fly back northward to start their families and settle down – as do people who come to you looking for solid ground.

The bees and butterflies begin to gather nectar from the first flowers of the season and others seek you for wisdom when they can find no rhyme or reason.

April showers bring May flowers. Just like winter brings snow. When you enter the room you take control and help others bloom and grow!

They know that you are the beginning point as you inspire them to seize their dreams. WOW - your tenacious manner motivates them to dig in until they beam.

The month of April is the beginning of planting time in this world – so continue to be that fertile soil where souls can take hold of new beginnings and flourish – You're that golden girl!

Go ahead and shine – don't worry about what gets left behind – seek God's kingdom first for all you need will be provided at birth - yes even the sod! For you to lie and rest in his love to wake again and flourish high above!

ARE YOU WHO HE WANTS TO BE?

When your child looks in your eyes does he see who he wants to be?

Does he see a person of honor and one of integrity?

Does he see the love of God enforced through love and a disciplined heart?

Does he strive to emulate your example no matter how hard?

To stand tall when life's promises look short? To be brave in spite of the pain?

Or does he look to accomplish much just to receive the gain?

Does he long to please you at any cost? Or does he sometimes seem lost?

Your child is your reward from God a gift of love you see

Make sure the man he sees in you is the man you want him to be.

BLACK BEAUTY

- You shine like a pearl made of glitter and gold – formed from birth to bring his Glory to my soul
- Black Beauty – your worship is so pure – Black Beauty your love is so dear
- Your praise rings brilliantly through my ear – No other sound is as clear
- His eye is on the sparrow He watches you from afar – how precious in His name you are
- Smile in anticipation – you are his glorious creation
- To see you praise without shame – to hear you glorify his name
- Oh how He loves to see your face – to watch you honor Him and receive His grace
- Black Beauty – no other does he adore – no other's voice does he so enjoy
- The sweet melody that moves through your lips – a precious gift to your master – not one beat does it skip – a motion so powerful – it could move ships
- Black Beauty keep praising His name and doing His will so that the world may know Him still!

COME REMEMBER WITH ME

I REMEMBER WHEN I HAD NO SHOES – ONLY
THE BLUES BECAUSE I HAD NO FOODS

I REMEMBER WHEN I SLEPT WITH MY FIVE
OTHER SISTERS AND BROTHERS.

 BUT I WAS LOVED BY MY MOTHER

I REMEMBER WHEN I DIDN'T HAVE ANY LUNCH

I COULDN'T RUN WITH THE ELITE BUNCH

BUT I HAD GRACE AND MERCY AND FAVOR

BECAUSE OF MY GODLY BEHAVIOR

I REMEMBER WHEN I LOST MY JOB – ALL I
COULD DO WAS SOB

I COULDN'T GET IT BACK, AND ALL I HAD WAS
LACK.

I REMEMBER WHEN I WAS IN DEBT AND COULD
NOT GET MY OBLIGATIONS MET.

I LIVED BY GRACE FROM MONTH TO MONTH

NEVER KNOWING HOW OR WHY

NO MATTER HOW DESPARATE I GOT, I KNOW
NOW THAT GOD HEARD MY CRY.

SO I TURNED TO THE WORD - SEEMS LIKE I'D
HEARD IT BEFORE

I READ IT AND RECITED IT – SOMETIMES WHILE
LYING ON THE FLOOR.

IT SAID TO ME "SEEK HIM FIRST" AND THE
MORE I READ THE MORE I'D THURST

FOR TRUTH AND KNOWLEDGE AND GUIDANCE
YOU SEE, I NEEDED TO FIND THE REAL ME.

IT SAID THAT GOD'S WORD WOULD NEVER
COME BACK VOID –

 IT SAID THAT HIS WORD WAS SHARPER THEN
ANY TWO-EDGED SWORD.

I WAS FLOORED BY THE OUTCOME – COULDN'T
BELIEVE MY EYES

IT BROUGHT ME FROM DEATH AND PUT JOY IN OUR LIVES.

I ATE IT AND SLEPT IT AND CALLED IT BY NAME

I SOMEHOW SENSED THESE VERY WORDS WOULD TAKE ME TO FAME

NO, NOT MONEY OR DIAMONDS OR PEARLS

BUT PEACE - BEYOND THE UNDERSTANDING OF THE WORLD.

I REMEMBER IT ALL NOW – WITHOUT SADNESS OR GRIEF

BUT WITH A FEELING OF PASSION THAT IS SUCH A RELIEF.

I REMEMBER NOW HOW THOSE WORDS HELPED ME GROW

HELPED ME GO WHERE GOD WANTED ME TO GO.

HOW SWEET IT IS TO BE IN HIS FACE – LIVING BY MERCY AND FAVOR AND GRACE

WILLING AND OBEDIENT – EATING THE BEST OF THE LAND

BECAUSE I GAVE GOD MY HEART AND NOT JUST MY HAND.

MY FRIEND

- I played in the yard with my friend today –
  What joy and peace we had through play.
- She is the kind of friend who doesn't demand
  much – But gives the world with just one look
  – just one touch.
- Our friendship has grown over the years.
  We've shared some good times and some tears.
- But through it all we have matured and grown.
  We've developed a kind of gift that to many is
  not known.
- You see we know what the other needs – and
  because we are gardeners – we just plant the
  seeds.
- Then we allow God to do the rest – after all he
  knows best.
- He has guided us through our friendship
  journey – watching closely as we grew
- Making sure we kept our motives true.
- We've found this bond that weathers every
  storm. It's almost magic – way different from
  today's norm.
- Even when we haven't seen each other in a
  while. The greeting is always with a smile.
- We are quite different in a lot of ways – But
  just the same on these special days.
- Just like me she's happy to play all to herself.
  But she's perfect with others like a portrait on a
  shelf.
- Very dependable and kind – glad to say she's a
  friend of mine!

- We just play in the yard without a fuss. No drama no muss
- We talk and compare day to day notes. Neither of us is the kind to gloat.
- Our stories are simple you see. All about love and life and family.
- What a joy to have a friend – whom you can trust through thick and thin.
- Someone who will always be there
- To laugh and play and meet again – any time I need a friend.

COURAGE

Courage makes us choose the harder right instead of the easier wrong

It never allows us to be content with half of the truth when the whole truth can be won.

Courage endows us with the strength that is born of loyalty.

It is a noble cause to all, worthy of the chase, it serves with truth as it base.

It keeps no fear, in secrecy, especially when truth and right are in jeopardy

DEATH TO SELF

DEATH TO SELF INCREASES SPIRITUAL HEALTH

KILLING THE I'S WILL KEEP YOU ALIVE!

TO KILL THE ME'S STAY ON YOUR KNEES

NOW MURDER THE "MINE – YEAH – YOU ARE DOING JUST FINE!

DEATH TO SELF INCREASES SPIRITUAL HEALTH

JUST LIKE GIVING ALWAYS INCREASE YOUR WEALTH!

DON'T ASK ME TO SUFFER

I'LL TAKE A BULLET FOR YOU

BUT DON'T ASK ME TO SUFFER

I'LL DIE FOR YOU BUT I'LL NEED A BUFFER

I'LL GO THE DISTANCE BUT I CAN'T FINISH THE RACE

DON'T ASK ME TO LOOK YOU IN THE FACE!

I'LL DO WHAT I CAN WITHOUT THE STRAIN

I'LL DO WHAT I CAN AS LONG AS THERE IS NO PAIN

I'LL FOLLOW YOUR LEAD TO THE ENDS OF THE EARTH

I'LL GO ALL THE WAY WITH YOU FOR WHAT IT'S WORTH

DON'T ASK ME TO GIVE UP MY COMFORT, MY SAFETY, MY SPACE

I'LL BE RIGHT BEHIND YOU – YES – THAT'S THE RIGHT PLACE

A SOLDIER I'M NOT – BUT I'LL BE JOHNNY ON THE SPOT

I'LL STICK BY YOU LIKE A FRIEND – BESIDE YOU TO THE END

CLOSER THAN ANY BROTHER HAS BEEN

DON'T ASK ME TO SUFFER

DON'T MAKE ME FEEL PAIN

I NEVER SAID I WAS YOUR JOHN WAYNE

JESUS IS YOUR SAVIOR- HE'S THE ONE WHO DIED

HE'S THE ONE WHO WILL STICK CLOSE BY YOUR SIDE

SOME PEOPLE SAY THEY WILL DIE FOR YOU

THEY GIVE YOU THEIR HAND BUT NOT THEIR HEART

AS LONG AS IT'S SAFE, THEY'LL DO THEIR PART

THEY'LL STAND RIGHT BEHIND YOU WHILE YOU TAKE ALL THE RISK

FOR REASONS THEY WON'T COME FORTH – JUST CHECK THEIR LIST.

NO WEAPON FORMED AGAINST YOU WILL PROSPER THEY'LL SAY

I'VE GOT YOUR BACK – I'M WITH YOU ALL THE WAY

BUT DON'T ASK ME TO SUFFER – I JUST CAN'T TAKE THE PAIN

PLEASE – DON'T ASK ME TO SUFFER I'M NOT LOOKING FOR FAME

NOT EVERY MAN WILL GIVE UP HIS LIFE FOR A FRIEND

ONLY THOSE WHO ARE WILLING TO STAY WITH YOU THROUGH THICK OR THIN!

SO DON'T ASK ME TO SUFFER MY FREEDOM, MY PRIDE

FOR ONLY GOD STAYS THAT CLOSE BY YOUR SIDE.

DON'T OPEN THE GATES

Do not open the Gates

That's a door for Satan to enter

Don't open the Gates

He'll slip into your center

Don't open the gates

They just give the enemy a chance

To come into your spirit and change the music of your

dance.

DREAM ON

Job 33:14-17; 1 Kings 17:17; Ezekiel 40:4a; Isaiah 1:10; Nehemiah 8:3

On the hills of every dream there is a demon of doubt.

There is a devil on your shoulder whispering," what's this all about?"

No sooner is your dream conceived in your mind;

doubt and indecision in your heart you'll find.

Replace those thoughts with a smile or even a tear because God did not give you a spirit of fear. Pick up your pad and walk. Stop listening to all that negative talk.

Cry unto the Lord and your soul will come unto you again. (*1Kings 17:17*)

For I am your father, your brother, and your friend.

In a dream, in a vision of the night, I will give you twenty-twenty sight.(*Job 33:14-17*)

I will show you the way to go. I will tell you all you need to know.(*John 14:26*)

Behold, with thine eyes, hear with thine ear. (*Ezekiel 40:4*)

With my guidance what is there to fear? (*Nehemiah 8:3*)

Be patient, have faith in my word. (*Isaiah 1:10*)

Dream on, believe what you've heard.

No weapon formed against you shall prosper you see (*Romans 8:28*)

If I am the giver of the dream in thee.

Am I a man that I should lie? No dream from me shall ever die!

EAT More – Play Less

- Eat your veggies – they are good for you
- Isn't that what your mama said to do?
- God wants you to eat more of his word too
- His words are your vitamins – your strength untold
- His principles are what will make you bold
- Your bible is the blood that builds your marrow
- It holds the key to your great tomorrow
- Eat up – go ahead and fill up your cup
- Your spiritual muscles will be built up
- If only you would do his will – your spirit man will get his fill
- Don't play the "I'm full game" with God's word
- Keep eating it up – do what you've heard
- Practice hearing from God in all things
- Start experiencing the success that it brings
- Beat the flesh with the rod of his word
- It will build your character so I've heard
- Your spirit will be renewed if just this morning on his word you chewed
- If playing the "hid it under the plate game"
- Remember not eating the word will always put you to shame
- So eat it, chew it well
- The smile in your heart will tell the tale
- Don't stir it and move it around on your plate – trying to figure it out
- That is not what eating his word is all about
- Take small bites at first to taste the flavor

- You will immediately notice the changes in your behavior
- It will fuel your soul and make you whole – then your mind will line up with what it has been told.
- Be willing to go through the process – Eat more and play less

HOW DO YOU KEEP THE SMILE?

How do you keep the smile?

- The smile of a child
- A child who's safe – who is loved by the One from above
- A child who is free – to be all that he can be

How do you keep the smile?

- It seems to fade after a while
- After the love is gone
- After the last song – when
- No one seems to care any more
- When all your dreams have fallen to the floor
- Like misplaced notes they disappeared
- Never to return – not in a million years!
- Just tears and pain and grief?
- Will the smile return and bring much needed relief?

How do you keep the smile?

- Just look to the hills for the smile

- The glow of love and joy and peace – it comes from the East

- The smile that will touch your heart

- The smile that will never depart

- Put it on and wear it proud

- This smile will cause you to laugh out loud!

- With His smile no weapon formed against you can win

- 'Cause when you are with Him you are in like FLIN!

- NOW LAUGH MORE AND LOVE MORE TOO.

- Wear that smile? It looks so good on you!

I AM HERE

I AM NO ACCIDENT, MY CREATION WAS NOT AN AFTER THOUGHT

WITH HIS BLOOD I WAS PURCHASED AND BOUGHT

I was created on purpose by my father to fulfill a void in this world. Therefore, my being here at this place at this time is as significant as an oyster is to a pearl

I am key to the success of this operation.

I am not here to be on vacation but to contribute to someone's salvation.

I am here because God created me for such a time as this.

So that a soul's chance for freedom will not be missed.

I am here to answer a question posed by an unsure, uncertain heart

I am here to function to give to do my predestined part

I am not here to steal your thunder – to point out or highlight your blunder

I am here to build you up and make your burden a little lighter. To make your day shine a little brighter

I am here for God created a universe with different parts

To be shaped and played out together from his collection of different hearts.

I am here – so don't try and change me into your vision of what you think I should be

I am here 'cause I was created by the "Great I AM" just for thee!

I ASKED THE LORD TO BLESS YOU

I ask the Lord to bless you, as I pray for you today,

to guide you and protect you, as you go along your way.

God's love is always with you, God's promises are true.

And when you give God all your cares, you know God will see you through – author unknown

Just pass this little blessing to someone you know today,

So God can take their cares away as they work and play.

The thought will make you smile, the action will build you up

'Cause when you give it away, it comes back to fill your cup! –

I PRAYED FOR YOU

I prayed for you the other day

I told God to have his way

To make you whole again

Because you are my dear friend

I asked him to heal your body and ease your pain

So that you can be free again

To be a father, a husband a grandpa and friend

But most of all because you obey his command

You've taken his word throughout the land

You've brought his word to those in need

You've always stood willing and ready to plant his seed

So he told me not to worry and not to fret

He said you were his friend too and that your healing is a sure bet!

"In loving memory of Deacon Curtis Patton – 2014"

I Wish You Enough!

I wish you enough sun to keep you bright
No matter how dark is your night

I wish you enough pain to fall in love
This is a passionate plea from above

I wish you enough joy to keep you alive
No matter how tough is for you to survive

I wish you enough gain to satisfy your desire
No need to ask or inquire

I wish you enough pain to keep you awake
No matter how troublesome the ache

I wish you enough loss to remind you of your own
No need to groan or cry and moan

I wish you enough hellos to light your eye
No matter how heavy the final good-bye

IT'S OKAY TO BE OKAY!

It's OK to be Okay – to be like Christ is the only way.

It's OK to be Okay-Just like Jesus is how you want to stay.

Don't feel ashamed because you serve in His name. You were created to win life's game

It's OK to be Okay - He gave you life to live for him to keep the weary from feeling dim.

To defeat dark days with all your might – you are the salt – you are the light.

You'll take on their sorrow, like Christ took on our sin, but like Him you will rise to fight again.

Stand up tall, be brave in the fight; let everyone know from whom you get your might.

Shout to the world the victory song – He is my savior my whole life long

Christ is the one with the power you see, He died and rose again to give it to me.

I share in His power and His suffering too – for I am now a son of the father too.

I'll keep planting that seed and doing good deeds

By faith I will march on 'cause with God's help I will stay strong!

He said he would never leave me nor ever forsake me; and no weapon formed will ever over take me.

So I set my face like flint – even though I may get bruised or bent

Like Him I may suffer, but like Him I will rise to take the everlasting prize

Of fellowship with God – on his right hand I stand to show the world that he is ruler of this land.

It will be Okay as He guides my way to fellowship again – with Him as my friend.

It's OK to be Okay – Christ like for others is the best way today!

No fear – no fret just basking in His righteousness!

JESUS ON YOU

HE IS MY JOY

Joy in the time of sorry

Joy in the time of peace

Joy in the midst of trouble

Joy in the midst of victory

Joy in the middle of bad history.

HE IS MY JOY!

Joy when I'm in the fight

Joy in the middle of the night

Joy when I'm on Top

Joy when the world says I flopped

Joy when I'm under attack

Joy 'cause He's got by back

Joy when I'm up

Joy 'cause I believe and I receive

HE IS MY JOY!

JESUS ON YOU IS YOUR JOY!

MOVING FORWARD

Your life is your garden; your thoughts are the seeds.

If your life isn't awesome, you've been watering the weeds.

So sing a new song – in worship is where you belong.

Do a new dance – this is your second chance!

Moving Forward – making all things new – Your past is over – your worries are now few.

Cleansed from your past – you are free – free at last!

God loves you – he is your example – your camels are loaded – your blessings are more than ample.

No longer crushed – no longer bruised – no longer feeling unwanted and used.

Moving Forward in grace and peace – Standing tall not looking back

Standing bold – no longer under attack!

Lay your cares at His feet – you are no longer in retreat – Our God cannot and will not be beat!

Moving Forward – I have enough for me and my "*sista*" too!

MOVING FORWARD – is my father's will - now that is what I'll do!

MY WISH FOR YOU

I wish you the joy of a sun shiny day

The push of a warm breeze to carry you on your way

The rain to wash away your tears and a close friend to calm your fears

I wish God's favor in all that you do, God's grace to energize and see you through

His power to overcome the obstacles at hand

His Spirit to guide your every plan

I wish you discipline to stay the course and keep the faith

The courage to accept the challenge and stay in the race.

I wish you wisdom to make decisions that are in His will

The knowledge that His love will see you through and keep you safe from life's issues both old and new.

I wish you insight to appreciate the rain and know its purpose although it may bring you pain

To see the Son as the guiding light that will bring you joy during your darkest night.

NO HILL FOR A CLIMBER

Ain't no hill for a climber

God himself is the timer

The road will be rough

The going will get tough

All tests look like troubles

But they're only opportunities wrapped in little bubbles

They build up your character and make you a man

They let you know you live in the "I can".

I can't is not a choice

You are now our voice

We will look to you for advice, and we won't

Hesitate to ask you twice

You promised to give it your all,

You humbled yourself and answered the call.

So be strong my brother because there is no other

Who could handle our cause?

With vigor and valor and without pause!

Don't be rushed by those who make a fuss

They had their turn, now you can work to earn.

The respect of the people, a love for this great land

The Grace of God and his loving hand!

AN AMERICAN MAN

I saw a man in the hall today

Half of his arm was blown away

He had an iron hook for a hand

But he stood tall and strong

He was An American man!

He smiled as I passed him by

I could clearly see the pain in his eye

It seemed as if his life had stopped

He went to the store but he had not shopped

For the life left in his hand

This tall strong American man

I smiled and nodded as my heart cried out to say

I know your pain –it will soon go away.

If you need a friend I extend my heart

To thank you for doing more than your part

This sacrifice of love is a gift that

Could only come from above

As your sister in arms and in Christ's Name, I pray

That your peace will soon return again someday!

MILITARY WOMAN

FROM STEEL TOED BOOTS TO HIGH HEELED SHOES

THE MILITRY WOMAN PAYS HER DUES.

SHE DEFENDS HER COUNTRY ON FOREIGN LAND, AND CAN

STILL HANDLE HOME, CHILDREN, AND HER MAN.

GOD IS HER CENTER, HER FOUNDATION AND HER COVER

HE GIVES HER JOY AND PEACE LIKE NO OTHER!

SHE IS THE GREATEST THING SINCE SLICED BREAD. YOU SEE

SHE COULD EVEN BE A STAR ON TV.

SHE COMES PREPARED TO PASS THE TEST NO
MATTER WHAT

OR WHO CREATED THE MESS.

ALWAYS READY WITH HER BAGS PACKED.

NEVER CONCERNED HOW THE CARDS ARE
STACKED.

A MILITARY WOMAN IS WHAT YOU NEED TO

CATCH THE DUDE WHO DID THE DEED!

911 IN REVIEW

Ten years ago we were moving kind of slow. - A nation at peace with itself.

We needed to move, to grow, to change but we just put those thoughts on a shelf.

After 200 years surely all our dues had been paid. So we went on our way - forgetting the Covenant with God that we'd made.

We had been untouchable from birth PAUSE - WHY – "We are the greatest nation on earth!

PAUSE - And then it happened – they came to us - to kill - to steal, and destroy – that peaceful slumber we had come to enjoy.

They used our sense of security and power to bring down both of those towers.

They killed innocent people just like lambs at the slaughter – and we immediately turned to revenge – just like any super power ought to!

We put on all of our armor, gassed up our tanks, and lined up our planes – these guys would never touch us again!

We sent the youngest, the biggest, the brightest in the land; it seemed as though our future was slipping right out of our hands. I heard a voice say – "Turn from your wicked ways and I will hear from heaven and heal this land and increase your days".

Yes, we brought back the plunder – Mr. Ben Laden himself. But we didn't find our peace on that shelf.

We spent so much in money and people's lives. It was like stinging a bee in his own hive. PAUSE - For what, to prove that no one messes with the power – no one can match us – in our finest hour?

Now as we try to mourn our loss, trying hard to remember, to count the cost – we check every corner, we're shaking with dread. PAUSE It turns out more than our soldiers were dead. We've lost our serenity, our security and peace, PAUSE - will we ever get it back - or our sanity at least?

Will we ever return to those days of old, when America was the home of the free, the proud, and the bold? Will we once again be able to look our children in the eyes and tell of a time that we truly enjoyed a day with blue skies?

PAUSE - Our God of hope says that we can be there again. We can love and smile and run with the wind! We can get our feet back on solid ground, as long as we are willing to keep him around.

If my people, he says, who are called by my name will humble themselves and pray, I am the one, the truth and the light, and I will make them pay, for vengeance is mine and only I know the way.

So turn, I say from your wicked ways, and this ambiguity will end. For no greater love has any man than to give up his life for a friend.

A BLACK MAN IN THE WHITE HOUSE

A Black Man in the White House,

"What You Say!"

A Black Man in the White House,

That'll be the day.

When America returns to its dream

Of Living and dying together

As one united Team

Moving closer to what life in America should mean

A Black Man in the White House

"What you say?"

A Black Man in The White House?

"Yes, That will be today."

When all of God's Children – Black, White, Yellow, and Brown

Will come together – they won't be let down.

We will again rule the world and say to the earth

That God's hand has been on us – even before our birth.

A black man in the white house – What you say?

A black man in the white house – that'll be the day.

Our forefathers will sing – "Let freedom ring,

One nation under God".

We have finally returned to our place above

In concert with God in truth and love.

A Black Man in the white house,

"What You Say?"

A Black Man in the White House,

Yes – That will be the today!

CHANGE IN AMERICA

- Change in America – That was the Theme
- What does it really mean?

- When things are so lost and our pockets so lean
- What do we do now – Holy cow!

- Where do we go – our jobs are gone and
- Our economy is so slow!

- Change in America – who will take the lead
- Who will chain the guy who did this dirty deed?

- How do we capitalize on this great opportunity?
- To move back to a state of total integrity

- So that we can show our children we really do care
- And leave them a legacy that will permanently be there!

- When their children are grown and ready for leading
- They won't have to call on other nations neither begging or pleading

- We will put this country back on solid ground
- And leave them a heritage made up of black, white, and brown.

- No matter the price

- We will return to a place where it's ok to be nice.

BIOGRAPHY

Margaret Gilbert is a wife, mother, grandmother and great-grandmother. After serving in the United States Air Force for over 30 years, she retired as the Command Chief Master Sergeant of the 118th Airlift Wing, located in Nashville, Tennessee. Growing things is her passion, therefore, being selected to serve and develop the airman population of the 118th Airlift Wing came natural to her. She believes that one of the purposes for her creation was to serve others and help them reach their maximum potential through inspiration, encouragement and teaching them to practice sound life principles based on the word of God.

A native of LaVergne, TN she holds a Bachelor's Degree in Human Resource Management from Trevecca Nazarene University and a Masters of Education with a concentration on Adult Education from Strayer University. Mrs. Gilbert currently serves as a Deacon at the Living Truth Christian Center in Smyrna, TN where she is the Dean of the Kingdom Living Institute. The institute offers education opportunities to adult partners as well as members of the surrounding community. *"Graciously Growing Greatness in Redemptive Love"* is the motto that inspires her to continue in her quest to help others use their God- given gifts to maximize their potential.

"Graciously Growing Greatness in Redemptive Love - GGGRL"

Made in the USA
Charleston, SC
24 November 2014